First Ladies: The Life and Legacy of Dolley ...

By Charles River Editors

About Charles River Editors

Introduction

Dolley Madison (1768-1849)

"It is one of my sources of happiness never to desire a knowledge of other people's business." – Dolley Madison

American presidents have shaped the course of global affairs for generations, but as the saying goes, behind every great man there's a great woman. While the First Ladies often remain overshadowed by their husbands, some have carved unique niches in their time and left their own lasting legacy. Dolley Madison helped establish the role of the First Lady in the early 1800s, Eleanor Roosevelt gave voice to policy issues in a way that made her a forerunner of First Ladies like Hillary Clinton, and Jackie Kennedy created glamorous trends that made her more popular than her husband. In Charles River Editors' First Ladies series, readers can get caught up to speed on the lives and legacies of America's most famous First Ladies in the time it takes to finish a commute, while learning interesting facts long forgotten or never known.

After the Constitution was ratified, George Washington went about setting all the precedents for the role of the presidency, establishing traditions like the Cabinet. But the role of being the First Lady of the United States was defined by the wife of the 4th president. James Madison may have been the Father of the Constitution, but his wife Dolley all but defined the responsibilities and customs of being the president's wife. Dolley had served as an informal First Lady for the widowed Thomas Jefferson, but when her husband entered the White House in 1809, Dolley went about furnishing the White House to such an extent that much of the style and items she chose were still in place when Mary Todd Lincoln became the First Lady in 1861. Dolley also became a folk hero of sorts and the center of a colorful legend that had her saving Gilbert Stuart's priceless painting of George Washington just ahead of the British while her husband was denigrated for fleeing as Washington D.C. was burned.

In addition to being instrumental in decorating the White House, Dolley Madison also set the standard for the First Lady's traditional hosting and ceremonial duties. 150 years later, Jackie Kennedy was largely credited for helping boost her husband's popularity during their time in the White House, but the same could easily be said about Dolley, who was renowned for her social graces and her hospitality. Having helped boost her husband's popularity during his presidency, Dolley went about maintaining his legacy after 1836, collecting and organizing the papers and notes of the Constitution's most influential drafter, and eventually selling them to the government in full.

First Ladies: The Life and Legacy of Dolley Madison looks at the life and legends of one of America's most influential First Ladies. Along with pictures of important people, places, and events in her life, you will learn about Dolley Madison like you never have before, in no time at all.

Sketch of Dolley, 1800

Chapter 1: Dolley Payne

Nothing could have been more inauspicious about the birth of early America's most famous hostess than her birth. Dolley Payne Todd was born to Mary and John Payne on May 20, 1768. The Paynes were a Quaker couple who were very devoted to their faith. Mary had been born and raised in the Meeting of friends, while John had converted in order to marry her. However, as is often the case with converts, his piety soon outdid hers. Though both the Paynes were born and raised in Virginia, when Dolley was born they were living with in New Garden, North Carolina, with their two sons, Walter and William Temple. One of the few questions from this time period is exactly how Dolley's name was truly spelled. Though historians have settled on Dolley, she wrote Dolly in her will, and records from the 18th century suggest her name was spelled Dollie.

It seems that Mary Cole was not happy in North Carolina and missed her family, so in 1768 John moved his wife and now four children back to Virginia, where they lived on a large, comfortable plantation in Hanover County, Virginia. Like his neighbors, John Payne farmed for a living with the help of a large staff of slaves, most of whom he had inherited from his own family or his wife's.

With that, a major issue arose for the devout Quaker family. The Quakers in America strongly disapproved of slavery and spoke out regularly in opposition to the practice. While John Payne's conscience became increasingly troubled by consistencies between what he believed and what he did, he had several other concerns that delayed him doing anything about them. First, he had a large family to support that would come to include eight children. Then there was the American Revolution, and the Payne plantation spent much of the period between 1775 and 1783 in a constant state of fear that fighting would come so near their home that they would be injured or forced out. Making matters more difficult, since the Quaker Paynes were pacifists, there was also suspicion on both sides that they actually supported the enemy. By the time the war ended in 1783, John Payne had made his decision and freed his slaves, sold his plantation, and moved his rural born and bred family to the bustling city of Philadelphia.

From what we know of Dolley's later life, it is easy to surmise that colonial Philadelphia must have been like a dream come true for her. Here she might pass by the famous Benjamin Franklin while doing her family's marketing, or see George Washington's coach pass by while her family was walking to Meeting. For a girl who'd known very few people other than her immediate family, just making friends and meeting fellow Quakers was a thrill.

Unfortunately, John Payne did not find Philadelphia as much to this liking. As a farmer, he had known how to grown a healthy crop, store it correctly to feed his family, and sell off the excess for a profit. However, there were no farms in Philadelphia, so he opened a business making and selling starch, which it turned out he knew nothing about. When the business failed six years later, he was forced to admit before the Quaker meeting that he had debts he was unwilling to pay. The final blow came when these very people, whom he had given up all for, turned their backs on him and "read him out of meeting," excommunicating him.

Chapter 2: Dolley Payne Todd

With her father bankrupt, 18 year old Dolley quickly realized that the best thing she could do for her parents was to help them have one less mouth to feed. Thus it was that the beautiful and care-free girl married the strict and serious minded John Todd in 1790. In spite of their differences, the two seemed to have been happy together, and the young family soon expanded to include a son, little John Payne Todd. The household grew even more by taking in Dolley's sister, Anna, who they supported in order to take some of the financial burden off the Paynes.

Miniature of Dolley, painted by James Peale, 1794

Sadly, young Dolley would not have to worry about her father much longer. John Payne died in 1792, having never recovered from the shock of losing his business and church in such quick succession. Without him to stand in her way, Dolley's sister Lucy quickly became engaged to George Washington's nephew, George Steptoe Washington. When the two married in 1792, she joined her father on the soon to be long list of Payne family members who were dismissed from the Quaker church.

Left a young widow with eight children to provide for, Mary Payne originally tried running a boarding house, renting out rooms that were no longer filled with her children to men coming to Philadelphia to meet with the Federal Congress. However, when a Yellow Fever epidemic struck Philadelphia in 1793, her boarders abandoned their quarters and returned to their homes, or at least to stay with family or friends outside the city. While a more established business might have been able to survive this economic downturn, Mary Payne was not. Realizing that she could not make enough money to support herself and her two youngest children, she sold the house in 1793 and took them to live with Lucy and her husband.

While the fever epidemic took a financial tool on her mother, for Dolley it proved to be devasting. Still recovering from the birth of her second child, William Temple, three months earlier, she was in no condition to survive an attack of fever. Concerned for her welfare, and that of the children, John Todd took her and the boys to stay with friends outside of town. John refused to stay behind safely himself, however, and instead returned to nurse fellow Quakers and others who had fallen ill in the city.

Tragically, Todd contracted the fever himself and, weakened by his hard work caring for others, quickly succumbed. A few days later, their youngest son, baby William, also died. Father and son were buried together in the graveyard of the old Quaker meeting house in Philadelphia, while his two year old son and 25 year old widow now faced a life without him.

Chapter 3: Dolley Payne Todd Madison

All accounts of Dolley at this time indicate the she was exceptionally pretty, with dark curly hair, dancing blue eyes and a soft, slightly plump figure. As a widow with a young child, everyone who knew her expected her to re-marry soon, and one by one many of her Quaker brethren came calling on her. Some of these Quakers had never married, others had lost their wives to childbirth or the epidemic, but Dolley no doubt caught their eyes. Nevertheless, Dolley spurned them all, turning her attention instead to the type of men she met at her sister Lucy's lovely home.

Why was Dolley so disinclined to attach herself again to a Quaker, as her church expected? There are probably several reasons. Dolley may very well have blamed the end of her prosperous, comfortable childhood on the Quakers' teaching against slavery, and she could have harbored resentment at the way the Quakers had treated her father in his time of need. Dolley might have even felt that it was her own husband's greater sense of duty toward the members of their congregation than toward his family that cost him his life and the life of her baby, leaving her a widow. Finally, she may have simply looked around the bustling town she lived in, with all the beautiful clothes and fine houses and thought to herself that there was more to life than hard work and Quaker gray.

Aaron Burr

Whatever her reasons, there's no doubt Dolley found herself very popular whenever she visited Lucy. One of the men she met during this time was U.S. Senator Aaron Burr, who was unattached and would show up for a cup of tea and an afternoon of conversation. It was during these talks that Dolley discovered the fascinating world of politics which her father had so seriously eschewed. However, while she loved politics, she soon made it clear that she did not, and would not, love Mr. Burr. It would be Burr's friend James Madison who asked Burr to introduce him to Dolley, and it was he who managed to turn her head when Burr brought him one day.

James Madison

One might well wonder why a bachelor paying a call on a lady would bring along another man. However, when taking into account that Madison was 17 years older than Dolley, already balding and just barely five feet tall, it might have been that Burr wouldn't have ever considered him a romantic rival. Dolley, however, thought otherwise, and soon the two had formed a romantic attachment. The two met in May 1794, and after a very brief courtship they were engaged in August and married on September 15, 1794.

Madison may have had physical shortcomings, at least in a modern sense, but he also represented a future that reminded Dolley of her past. In addition to being one of the nation's influential politicians and the Father of the Constitution, Madison was a wealthy Virginian just as her father had been, and without Quaker teachings to bother his conscience he was likely to stay that way. Dolley may in fact have considered the day she too was "read out of meeting" for marrying outside the faith to be one of triumph rather than tragedy.

For his part, finally making Dolley his wife must have been a tremendous relief for Madison. Though modern history sees him as an old man in a powdered wig, he was, like the rest of the Founding Fathers, a real flesh and blood man with the same longings as any man of today. In a letter that certainly would have shocked her mother, Dolley's cousin wrote to her:

...now for Mad---- he told me I might say what I pleased to you about him to begin, he thinks so much of you in the day that he has Lost his Tongue, at Night he Dreames of you & Starts in his Sleep a Calling on you to relieve his Flame for he Burns to such an excess that he will be shortly consumed & he hopes that your Heart will be callous to every other swain but himself he has Consented to every thing that I have wrote about him with Sparkling Eyes...

The newlywed Madisons continued to live in Philadelphia for the next three years, but Dolley quickly grew dissatisfied with his bachelor rooms and persuaded her husband to rent a large townhouse for themselves, little Payne, and the ever present Anna. With his wealth, she decorated it well in the latest style and with the most fashionable furnishings. And while she was at it, she decorated herself, buying an entire new wardrobe to replace her plain Quaker frocks, as well as suits, hats, boots and toys for Payne. Having had money for decades with no one to spend it on, Madison watched his young wife's antics with delight.

Throughout her life, Dolley would prove that she loved the finer things in life, but it would be unfair to suggest that the marriage was simply one of financial convenience. While Dolley certainly enjoyed his money, there is every indication that she loved Madison the man even more. For instance, when he retired from politics in 1797 to move back to Virginia and care for his elderly father, she appears to have gladly traded her new found life as a cosmopolitan hostess for the quiet life he longed for on the plantation. Though she was still not yet 30, she was content to be wherever he was, doing whatever he wanted to do.

What did Dolley see when she first rounded the corner and headed up the lane toward her new home? First, there was the 5,000 acres of land, most of it under cultivation. As her carriage drove to her new home, she passed by tall trees, some of which had pre-dated her arrival by a century. These included sagging weeping willows, sturdy walnut trees and long lengths of box hedge. Then there were the grape arbors, hanging heave with fruit and, over course, the ever present acres and acres of tobacco.

The enormous plantation had a large rolling lawn that led up to the stately brick home covered with delicate white limestone. Built by his father when James was just a boy, the most striking feature was the tall front portico, supported by four elegant columns. This provided a shady place to rest on summer afternoons and a safe place to wait for admittance during inclement weather. Behind the large house was an attached kitchen and dozens of small homes for the family's more than 100 slaves.

Montpelier, the Madisons' home

Inside, she discovered that both men had been busy preparing the home for its new lady. The light, airy rooms were hung with fashionable silk drapes and decorated with one of the finest art collections in the United States. The most basic furniture had been made by skilled artisans on the plantation or in nearby Williamsburg, but the Madisons imported the best pieces from France.

Chapter 4: Learning How To Be First Lady

Having moved to Montpelier in 1797, Dolley assumed traditional household management of the plantation and its slaves, as well as caring for her elderly mother-in-law.

Just as happened in Philadelphia, Dolley had little time to enjoy the fruits of her labor. Madison's close friend, political kindred spirit and near neighbor, Thomas Jefferson, was elected president in 1801. Since the constitution at that time stated that the runner up in an election would be Vice President, who just so happened to be Aaron Burr, Jefferson needed someone he trusted for the third in line slot, Secretary of State. He asked Madison who, after talking the offer over with Dolley, accepted. Thus, the family, including pretty 21 year old Anna, packed up again and moved to Washington, where they would end up living for the next 16 years.

Thomas Jefferson

If Dolley expected that same sort of bustling beauty that she'd seen in Philadelphia, she was sorely disappointed. In 1801, Washington D.C. was still a brand new town, created out of a political compromise that intended to move the seat of government to the South, and it was swampland that had never been fit to farm. The buildings that were already there were mostly incomplete, including the White House. However, Dolley seemed to see the whole experience as an adventure, and she quickly settled into the large house Madison rented for them not far from the White House. Furthermore, because Jefferson was a widower, she informally took on the role of surrogate First Lady.

Perhaps most disturbing to the ever fashion conscious Dolley was the lack of shops and dress makers. When her sister Anna married Richard Cutts in 1803, they moved to the more prosperous and well established city of Baltimore, prompting Dolley to write:

My dear Anna, if you will get me a light shawl a dozen yards of fashionable handsome broad ribbon, a pair or 2 of gloves to enclose to M[adison] & anything else which you know I want, I will immediately enclose you a bill on Moiland or Lewis, who both owe M[adison] money, for the amount of what you may think proper to buy me. I trust you will find Riggs or some other opportunity for the bonnet, &c.

Ironically, it was earlier in this same letter that Dolley shared the tragic news about Jefferson's younger daughter, which would in turn push her further into the social spotlight as the grief stricken family relied more on her to keep the wheels of the White House turning:

A letter from the President announced the death of poor Maria & the consequent Misery it has occasioned them all. This is among the many proofs my dr. Sister of the uncertainty of life! A girl so young, so lovely--all the efforts of her Father doctors & friends availed nothing.

Dolley wouldn't have been in the position she was without being Dolley Madison, but she also won the position thanks to her own talents for using hospitality to smooth the way for political understanding. While Jefferson's daughters were gracious hostesses within their own circle of friends, they were still too young and immature to appreciate the subtleties of protocol, diplomacy and tact. Since their father cared little for these issues himself, it fell on Dolley's willing shoulders to advance her husband's career and Jefferson's presidency by candlelight and garden party.

Unfortunately, even the gracious Dolley could not smooth out every situation. At a dinner party held on December 2, 1803, Jefferson broke protocol by escorting Dolley into dinner instead of Mrs. Merry, the wife of the British ambassador. In his report about the evening, the minister reported with horror:

"Mrs. Merry was placed by Mr. Madison below the Spanish minister, who sat next to Mrs. Madison. With respect to me, I was proceeding to place myself, though without invitation, next to the wife of the Spanish minister, when a member of the House of Representatives passed quickly by me and took the seat, without Mr. Jefferson's using any means to prevent it, or taking any care that I might be otherwise placed…among the persons (none of those who were of this country were the principal officers of the government except Mr. Madison) whom the President selected for a dinner which was understood to be given to me, was M. Pichon the French *chargé d'affaires*. I use the word *selected*, because it could not be considered as a diplomatic dinner, since he omitted to invite to it the Danish *chargé d'affaires*, who, with the Spanish minister, form the whole body."

Dolley herself, who was still learning the ropes of precedence, was oblivious to the uproar that had ensued and innocently invited the Merrys to another dinner at her home a few nights later. Out of either loyalty or ignorance, Madison copied Jefferson's behavior, setting off another flurry of reports. According to the Spanish minister who had also attended the White House fiasco:

"…until then my wife and I had enjoyed in the houses of Cabinet ministers the precedence of which we had been deprived in the President's house; but on this day the Secretary of State too altered his custom, without informing us beforehand of his resolution, and took to table the wife of the Secretary of the Treasury. This unexpected conduct produced at first some confusion, during which the wife of the British minister was left without any one giving her his hand, until her husband advanced, with visible indignation, and he took her to table."

Next, the ambassadors met to complete construct their own plan of retaliation:

"M. Yrujo, who is vanity itself, blew the flame more vigorously than ever. . . . He concerted reprisals with Mr. Merry, and it was agreed that whenever they should entertain the secretaries and their wives, they should take none of them to table, but should give their hands to their own wives. This resolution was carried out at a dinner given some days afterward by M. Yrujo. Mr. and Mrs. Merry were next invited by the Secretary of the Navy. Mrs. Merry refused; yet this minister, a very well-bred man, had so arranged things as to give her his hand. Apparently what had taken place at Mr. Madison's was thought harsh, and it was wished to bring Mr. and Mrs. Merry back to a reconciliation."

The scandal finally rose to such a level that it attracted the attention of the sitting government.

"The Cabinet took up the question, as reported in the newspaper of which I sent you an extract, and it was resolved that hereafter the President should give his hand to the lady who might happen to be nearest him, and that there should be no precedence. Mr. Merry was invited to a tea by the Secretary of War and by the Secretary of the Treasury. To avoid all discussion he wholly refused the first, and after accepting the second he did not come. Finally, New Year's Day gave another occasion for scandal. On this day, as on the Fourth of July, it is the custom to call upon the President; and even the ladies go there. This year neither Mme. Yrujo nor Mrs. Merry went, and the Marquis took care to answer every one who inquired after his wife's health, that she was perfectly well."

Then, as today, the papers could hardly wait to get involved:

"Since then Washington society is turned upside down; all the women are to the last degree exasperated against Mrs. Merry; the Federal newspapers have taken up the matter, and increased the irritation by sarcasms on the Administration and by making a burlesque of the facts, which the Government has not thought proper to correct."

Of course, Dolley had her own take on the states of affairs, her social life having been largely unaffected by the arguments. She wrote to her sister:

"We go on just as usual. We have had 2 parties this week Duval's & Dearborns-- tonight at Thorntons--tomorrow night here. Mrs. Loid, Mrs. Mason's sister, will be here with a sister of Mrs. Prentis Smith & the little circle left in the City. Kitty Murry is still in G. T. She & Mrs. ...send you a great deal of love.

Mrs. Pichon has been in Baltimore 2 weeks -- she moves to the Seven Buildings as soon as she returns. Mrs. Merry is still the same strange [mood] she hardly associates with any one--always riding on Horseback."

Finally, the war between Britain and France made its way into the battle over precedence when Napoleon sent his cousin to represent him on a trip to Washington.

The arrival of M. Bonaparte with his wife in the midst of all this explosion has furnished Mr. Merry with new griefs. The President asked M. and Mme. Bonaparte to dinner, and gave his hand to Madame. There was, however, this difference between the two cases,—the President had invited on this day, besides myself and Mme. Pichon, only the two Messrs. Smith and their wives, who are of Mme. Bonaparte's family. But when Mr. Merry heard of it, he remarked that Mme. Bonaparte had on this occasion taken precedence of the wife of the Secretary of the Navy. . . I am aware that with tact on the part of Mr. Jefferson he might have avoided all these scandals.

For a while, Dolley was relieved of worrying about Washington social wars, though not in a good way; she developed a serious abscess on her knee, and was forced to go to Philadelphia for several weeks for treatment. Her letter to her husband during this time gives insight into her strong feelings for him:

"A few hours only have passed since you left me, my beloved, and I find nothing can relieve the oppression of my mind but speaking to you, in this, the only way. Dr. Physic called before you had gone far, but I could only find voice to tell him my knee felt better. Betsey Pemberton and Amy (her maid) are sitting by me, and seem to respect the grief they know I feel at even so short a separation from one who is all to me. I shall be better when Peter returns with news, not that any length of time could lessen my first regret, but an assurance that you are well and easy will contribute to make me so. I have sent the books and note to Mrs. D. Betsey puts on your hat to divert me, but I can not look at her."

In addition to honing her hostess skills, Dolley used her exposure as Jefferson's called-upon First Lady to start moving in the necessary political and social circles that brought her into contact with Washington bigwigs. As a result, she was able to take on a large, public role raising funds to support the expedition by Lewis and Clark through the newly purchased Louisiana Territory.

By the time Jefferson's presidency was finished, Dolley was qualified to revolutionize the role of First Lady, changing it from one of simply being the president's wife to one that would later be called "Presidentress".

Chapter 5: First Lady Dolley Madison

Inauguration

Thanks to her work on behalf of Jefferson, Dolley was already a political asset before her husband even entered the White House. Her popularity as Washington's hostess was of incalculable value to her husband's campaign in 1808, and as a reflection of how central a role she had played in the White House, Federalist newspapers in Baltimore and Boston insinuated that Dolley had been romantically linked with President Jefferson as a way of attacking her and her husband. As it turned out, the Federalists had already unwittingly won their last presidential election with John Adams 12 years earlier, and Madison went on to capture the White House regardless of their attacks.

Dolley was set to shape the role of First Lady, but first she reshaped the presidential inauguration. In anticipation of her husband's inauguration on March 4, 1809, the commandant of the Washington Navy Yard, Captain Tom Tingey, asked Dolley to sponsor a dance and dinner. When she gladly accepted the request, she had just established the first presidential "inaugural ball". Held at Long's Hotel on Capitol Hill, 400 guests attended the party, and Dolley was anything but inconspicuous in a buff-colored velvet gown, wearing pearls and large plumes in a turban.

Renovating the White House

The Jefferson Administration may have had some issues with its party planning, but thankfully Dolley had learned the necessary lessons by the time her husband succeeded Jefferson in 1809. In fact, she was ready to take the city by storm, beginning right at the center of it all: the interior of the White House.

When Jefferson moved to Washington, he simply brought his own furniture to his new home, so he naturally took it all with him when he left. The Madisons certainly could have brought their own furniture, too, but Dolley had a better idea. She suggested that, since the president's mansion belonged to the people of the United States, so should its furniture. Working with architect Benjamin Latrobe, and his wife, she designed hundreds of items that would be used permanently in the public spaces of the mansion. These included tables of all sizes, chairs, drapes, stools and much, much more. Congress happily funded her project, knowing that Latrobe had a longstanding reputation for both the New World style and Old World grace of his structures. The trio worked tirelessly and pushed their workmen nearly to the breaking point.

Portrait of Latrobe, circa 1804

In her efforts, Dolley was aided by her newly widowed sister, Lucy Washington, who lost her husband just as Madison was taking office. Though a widow at 37 and the mother of four sons, she was like her sister in many ways and provided an excellent sounding board for issues from politics to decorating to entertaining. She was also a social star in her own right, and she soon found herself being courted by several men.

Hostess

All the hard work ultimately paid off when Dolley threw open the White House doors for her first public reception. While a few of her husband's opponents accused her of being a pretender, calling her an "innkeeper's daughter" and worse, the majority of the city's powerful people loved attending her parties, which were known for their simple elegance and style.

One of Dolley's favorite types of entertainment was what she called "drawing rooms." These were her own creations, combining the breadth of the levees hosted by predecessors with the informality of a family gathering. Whereas Martha Washington and Abigail Addams had remained securely entrenched in their formal receiving lines all evening, Dolley was more inclined to mingle, meeting both her husband's friends and enemies with the same grace.

At these events Dolley typically carried one of two items in her reticule. She might have a small book, not so that she could read, but so that she could show it to a guest and ask if he'd read it in the hopes of beginning a pleasant conversation around a neutral topic. On the other hand, she might have in her hand a small snuff box, from which she could offer her guests small pinches of powdered tobacco. While modern women might seem scandalized by this behavior, it was common practice among both men and women in the early 19th century.

Dolley also hosted regular "dove parties," where she invited the wives of congressmen to meet at the White House and discuss current events. While there is a myth among 20th century women that their female ancestors were not allowed to have political views, nothing could be further from the truth. While Dolley and her friends could not vote, that by no means meant they were uninterested or uninformed. These dove parties were popular and well attended, as Dolley gladly wrote to her sister Anna:

"All is bustle here electioneering yet. De Wit & the Smiths & I know not who all, intend to break us down. The Federalists [are] affronted to a man. Not one (I mean of the 2 houses of Congress) will enter M[adison']s door since the communication of (Henry) to Congress except Le Roy Livingston who considers himself attached by his appointment of Colonel to the Governor, General."

Finally, there were Dolley's famous dinner parties. An excellent cook in her own right, she was particularly adept at planning well-balanced menus. While it is true that many of these meals ended with a relatively new dish, ice cream, Dolley was not the first person to serve it in the White House; Thomas Jefferson was. However, she was more than happy to keep up the tradition, having blocks of ice cut from frozen northern lakes in the winter and stored in well insulated ice houses in Washington so her guests could enjoy the treat.

Perhaps Dolley's most delightful social event, however, was hosting sister Lucy Washington's wedding to Supreme Court Justice Thomas Todd in 1812. In a letter to their mutual sister Anna, she wrote:

"Before this reaches you Lucy will be married to Judge Todd of Kentucky! Yes, sudden as it is, we must be reconciled to it from her choice of a man of the most estimable character, best principles, & high talents. He is a widower with five children, one daughter married. The others [are] provided for and [are] not to live with them…in Lexington, very near our old friend, Taylor, where there is fine society and good schools for her children. In short, my dear Anna, though it breaks my heart to find myself left far from my sister, I rejoice at the husband she will have & the brother we shall acquire. As a supreme judge, he is obliged to come h[ere] for 2 months every winter & he binds himself to bring her to her friends when she pleases to come. They have appointed tomorrow week to be married & to go off for Hairwood next day, stay a week &, with the children, proceed to Lexington."

Creating a Public and Political Role

It's quite likely that Abigail Adams was the first wife of a president to act as a sounding board and informal advisor for her husband, but it was Dolley Madison who established the First Lady as a very visible and political role. As noted before, Dolley had renovated the White House in the hopes of making the changes permanent to reflect the fact that the public owned it. Now she went about establishing her role as one in which the citizens were her constituency as well. In doing this, Dolley ensured that the First Lady became an extension of her husband's administration as well.

Dolley used her position to improve the president's political fortunes in several ways. During parties, she would converse at length with Washington's politicians and spouses to learn their positions on critical political issues, or even attempt to persuade them of the benefits of Madison's views. Dolley was able to pull this off not only due to the grand but elegant style of the White House but thanks to her own personality, which made her guests feel at ease. In private, the First Lady exercised all political influence she could through correspondence and building relationships and personal alliances with politicians' wives, an objective she could help accomplish by having Madison provide supporters, friends and family members with government positions.

All of these responsibilities made the First Lady far more important among the corridors of power, but Dolley truly gave the First Lady a formally public role by formally associating herself with public and charitable projects. Having already proven an effective fundraiser, Dolley became a supporter and board member of a home in Washington, D.C. for young orphaned girls. Dolley also befriended nuns from a local Catholic school and formed an association with their organization, an incredibly unusual move since Americans in the late 18th and early 19th centuries who were descended from the British often harbored deep-seated prejudices against Catholics.

The Dolley Madison Legend

Dolley Madison was immensely popular, to a degree that her husband must have envied. President Madison found himself between a rock and a hard place concerning his foreign policy.

With talk of an alliance between Native Americans and the British on the Western Frontier, many members of Congress began to loudly call for war. In the midterm elections of 1810, a group of Congressmen committed to war with Britain had been elected. Led by Speaker Henry Clay, the group became known as the "War Hawks." With the knowledge gained from the Shawnee Wars, the War Hawks only began to call for war more loudly.

President Madison was under enormous pressure, and he was personally wavering on what to do. He supported the advice of President Washington and hoped to maintain neutrality. On the other hand, the British had continued to disrespect American neutrality, and were also threatening the nation's sovereignty and security in the West. Being unsure himself, Madison sent a message to Congress asking them to come up with a plan.

Even Congress was indecisive. They came up with a course of action, but it was not a broadly popular one. By a vote of 79 to 49 in the House, and 19 to 13 in the Senate, Congress offered President Madison a Declaration of War against Great Britain. The effort for war was led by Henry Clay and his largely Southern and Western War Hawk allies. In New England, the War of 1812 was enormously unpopular; the region had even continued some illegal trade with Great Britain despite the federal embargo. All 39 of the Federalists in Congress voted against war. It was a shaky start to the nation's first major military conflict. Regardless, President Madison accepted Congress' declaration on June 18th, 1812, starting the War of 1812.

At the same time, that declaration of war came in the midst of a tough reelection fight. Madison won reelection by a much smaller margin than he'd won in 1808, helped no doubt by his wife's popularity. Nevertheless, it was an indication of how unpopular "Mr. Madison's War" would prove to be.

With so many American families torn apart by the fighting, Dolley scaled back her entertaining and focused her energies instead on building morale and support for her husband's leadership. When she heard that the papers were calling it "Mr. Madison's war," she redoubled her efforts, smiling and bowing to everyone who called, whether they were friend or foe. She also made special efforts to visit the troops stationed around Washington, and to do what she could to assist their wives and children.

The War of 1812 is best known today for the burning of Washington and Andrew Jackson's victory at the Battle of New Orleans, which took place after the Treaty of Ghent had actually ended the war. However, the war would give rise to one of the most enduring legends of Dolley Madison's life. As the British prepared to invade the American capital in August 1814, Dolley wrote of the precarious situation for the Madisons during their last few days in the White House:

"Dear Sister

My husband left me yesterday morning to join Gen. Winder. He enquired anxiously whether I had courage, or firmness to remain in the President's house until his return, on the morrow, or succeeding day, and on my assurance that I had no fear but for him and the success of our army, he left me, beseeching me to take care of myself, and of the cabinet papers, public and private. I have since received two dispatches from him, written with a pencil; the last is alarming, because he desires I should be ready at a moment's warning to enter my carriage and leave the city; that the enemy seemed stronger than had been reported, and that it might happen that they would reach the city, with intention to destroy it. . . . . I am accordingly ready; I have pressed as many cabinet papers into trunks as to fill one carriage; our private property must be sacrificed, as it is impossible to procure wagons for its transportation. I am determined not to go myself until I see Mr. Madison safe, and he can accompany me, as I hear of much hostility towards him, ... Disaffection stalks around us. . . . My friends and acquaintances are all gone; Even Col. C with his hundred men, who were stationed as a guard in the enclosure . . . . French John (a faithful domestic,) with his usual activity and resolution, offers to spike the cannon at the gate, and to lay a train of powder which would blow up the British, should they enter the house. To the last proposition I positively object, without being able, however, to make him understand why all advantages in war may not be taken.

Wednesday morng., twelve o'clock. Since sunrise I have been turning my spyglass in every direction and watching with unwearied anxiety, hoping to discern the approach of my dear husband and his friends, but, alas, I can descry only groups of military wandering in all directions, as if there was a lack of arms, or of spirit to fight for their own firesides!

Three O'clock. Will you believe it, my Sister? We have had a battle or skirmish near Bladensburg, and I am still here within sound of the cannon! Mr. Madison comes not; may God protect him! Two messengers covered with dust, come to bid me fly; but I wait for him. . . . At this late hour a wagon has been procured, I have had it filled with the plate and most valuable portable articles belonging to the house; whether it will reach its destination; the Bank of Maryland, or fall into the hands of British soldiery, events must determine.

Our kind friend, Mr. Carroll, has come to hasten my departure, and is in a very bad humor with me because I insist on waiting until the large picture of Gen. Washington is secured, and it requires to be unscrewed from the wall. This process was found too tedious for these perilous moments; I have ordered the frame to be broken, and the canvass taken out it is done, and the precious portrait placed in the hands of two gentlemen of New York, for safe keeping. And now, dear sister, I must leave this house, or the retreating army will make me a prisoner in it, by filling up the road I am directed to take. When I shall again write you, or where I shall be tomorrow, I cannot tell!!"

Dolley did indeed get out of Washington in time, leaving dinner on the dining room table for her husband in case he should return in the night. However, she later learned that it was the British General who dined on her repast and then, after drinking a sarcastic toast to her with her own wine, proceeded to set fire to everything she had loved in her home.

As Dolley noted in letters to her sister, she successfully removed all kinds of invaluable papers and materials from the White House ahead of the advancing British, writing, "At this late hour a wagon has been procured, and I have had it filled with plate and the most valuable portable articles, belonging to the house…I am accordingly ready; I have pressed as many Cabinet papers into trunks as to fill one carriage; our private property must be sacrificed, as it is impossible to procure wagons for its transportation."

In the aftermath of the burning of much of Washington D.C. by the British, Dolley was celebrated for waiting until nearly the last minute to save General Stuart's priceless painting of George Washington, which she had hinted at in the letter to her sister.

Gilbert Stuart's "Lansdowne Portrait of George Washington". Dolley was credited with saving the White House copy of the painting from the White House

Gilbert Stuart

Though it may seem like a trivial side story among the overall narrative of the War of 1812, it burnished the legend of Dolley Madison and became a matter of controversy and intrigue during the 19th century. Historians noted that the letter in which Dolley mentions saving the painting exists only in a manuscript she had organized in the 1830s for an official biography, and that more contemporaneous letters written by Dolley at the time came across as far less stoic and brave.

In the mid-19th century, a man named Charles Carroll began publicly asserting that it was his father who had saved the Washington painting, drawing a direct response from Dolley, who wrote in 1848 that it was her idea to save the painting. "I directed my servants in what manner to remove it from the walls, remaining with them until it was done." One of the two men who Dolley identified as ultimately receiving the painting for safekeeping backed up her account, noting that Carroll's father had assisted in taking the painting down, but that it was done at Dolley's request. "As soon as our troops broke and retreated, the President sent his servant express to warn his good lady of her danger, with directions to leave immediately. . . . The messenger preceded me five or ten minutes, having passed me on the Pennsylvania avenue, and given the information, with a request that I would repair to the house and assist in their departure. . . . I acted at the special request of Mrs. Madison, and Mr. Depeyster co-operated with me in carrying her wishes into effect. I always supposed the praiseworthy solicitude originated with her; it would require very positive and clear proof to induce me to change that opinion. It certainly did not originate with me or with Mr. Depeyster; nor have I ever intimated that any other than Mrs. Madison was entitled to the least credit therefor."

Aside from Carroll's assertions, there seems to be a general consensus that it was Dolley's idea to save the painting, and that she directed some of her servants (including the one she identified as French John) to take the painting down, remove it from its frame, and move it. Historians believe one of the most objective accounts came from Paul Jennings, an enslaved servant in the White House who was in his teens at the time. In his memoirs, written half a century later, Jennings wrote, "It has often been stated in print, that when Mrs. Madison escaped from the White House she cut out from the frame the large portrait of Washington (now in one of the parlors there), and carried it off. This is totally false. She had no time for doing it. It would have required a ladder to get it down. All she carried off was the silver in her reticule, as the British were thought to be but a few squares off, and were expected every moment. John Susé (a Frenchman, then door-keeper, and still living) and Magraw, the President's gardener, took it down and sent it off on a wagon, with some large silver urns and such other valuables as could be hastily got hold of."

While Jennings agreed that Dolley had left before the work was done, his account is consistent with the notion that it was her idea and order to save the painting, thus entitling her to much of the credit she has historically received.

Paul Jennings

The war ended within months of the burning of Washington D.C., and the Madisons were back in Washington before the end of 1814. When they returned, they found a very hollowed out shell of the executive mansion.

George Munger's painting of the White House after it was burned in August 1814

The Octagon House

President Madison would spend the remainder of his term living in the Octagon House, but planning the necessary repairs to the White House was overseen by the First Lady. While she was never able to restore the interior to its pre-war glory, she was able to see the walls and windows repaired, as well as a fresh coat of white paint applied over the char marks of the fire. When looking at the President's home standing again in its original glory, people began to point out the "White House" as a symbol of national triumph. The name stuck and is still used to this day.

In addition to redecorating the White House, Dolley also devoted much of her time to caring for those left orphaned or destitute by the war. She turned her hospitality skills to fund raising events, such as concerts, orations and luncheons, that women were only too happy to attend, often contributing sizeable sums to her dearest causes. Following her lead, other women soon followed suit, and the Washington philanthropic organization was born.

Portrait of Dolley in 1817

Chapter 6: The First Lady of Montpelier

The remainder of Madison's term after the War of 1812 is viewed as largely successful and responsible for ushering in the Era of Good Feelings. Still, like his predecessors, Madison chose not to run for a third term, and in 1817 he and Dolley returned to Montpelier for a quiet retirement. For the next 20 years they would leave the plantation only rarely, usually for necessity, but they never visited Washington. Instead, they spent their time hosting those who came from Washington and the rest of the world to see them. Over time it came to be considered something a necessity for anyone wanting to have a career in politics to pay at least one formal call on the aging Madison and his pretty wife.

When not entertaining, the former president spent his time organizing his extensive record of the constitutional convention for publication. Dolley often helped with this project, reading aloud to him when his eyes tired or adding notes under his direction. She also placed items in the appropriate files and boxes so that they could be more easily found. Together, the Madisons ensured that the papers and notes he had taken and relied on for working on the U.S. Constitution would eventually be publicly available. Obviously, Madison's papers were an invaluable collection given his central role in writing the U.S. Constitution and Bill of Rights.

Delighting in each other's company, with enough work to keep James busy and enough company to delight Dolley, the two would have passed the final years of their marriage in complete peace had it not been for the ever looming spectre of financial troubles. Though the Madisons were extremely wealthy, they began to feel a financial pinch caused in part by economic shifts but primarily by Dolley's own son, Payne. In a letter she wrote to him in 1823, her disappointment that he had not written is palpable:

"I am impatient to hear from you at Philadelphia. My dearest Payne, had I known where to direct should have written to you before this--not that I had anything new to communicate, but for the pleasure of repeating how much I love you, & how much I wish to see you, & to hear of your happiness. Your Papa received the journal of Las Casas with your name in it, from Philadelphia, which was an indication that you are there, & I write accordingly."

The tragedy that was Payne Todd is a sad tribute to his mother's one major failing in life. She had spoiled him and could see no wrong in him, and it was now coming back to haunt the Madisons. When Payne was young and misbehaved, she wrote off his behavior to high spirits, rebuffing any efforts on her husband's part to discipline him or try shape his character. Later, when he was in college, he developed a taste for alcohol and gambling. Because his step-father was president of the United States, it was taken for granted that either he would have the money to pay his own debts, or Madison would pay them himself in order to avoid scandal.

The following year, Dolley again wrote her son, pleading with him to return home:

"I have received yours, my dearest Payne, of the 23d and 24th of November, and was impatient to answer them yesterday, the day of their reaching me, but owing to the winter arrangement for the mail, no post leaves this until to-morrow morning. Mr. Clay inquired affectionately after you ; he with two members of Congress have been passing several days with us. Everyone inquires after you ;

but, my dear son, it seems to be the wonder of them all that you should stay away from us for so long a time ! and now I am ashamed to tell, when asked, how long my only child has been absent from the home of his mother. Your father and I entreat you to come to us ; to arrange your business with those concerned, so that you may return to them when necessary, and let us see you here as soon as possible with your interest and convenience. Your father thinks as I do, that it would be best for your reputation and happiness, as well as ours, that you should consult your parents on subjects of deep account to you, and that you would find it so on returning to Philadelphia at the appointed time, which shall be when ever you wish it. I have said in my late letters, as well as this, all that I thought sufficient to influence you. I must now put my trust in God alone ! . . ."

Upon leaving college, his parents hoped that Payne might either study law or settle into the quiet life of a country planter. However, he did neither, preferring instead to travel about the country trading on his family's good name. Though they regularly sent him a substantial allowance, it was not enough to support his lavish lifestyle, and he piled up one debt after another.

The situation came to a climax in 1830, when Payne was finally convicted of not paying his bills and thrown in debtor's prison. Dolley, devastated at her son's plight, persuaded Madison to intervene. Whether or not she ever knew that he had to both sell off family-owned land in Kentucky and raise a mortgage on half their home remains uncertain. However, the funds were sent and Payne was released, but it soon became clear he hadn't learned his lesson.

Four years later, Payne appealed to his parents for even more money. Unable to borrow anything else on the plantation, Madison had no choice but to sell off several families of slaves. This grieved him more than any other loss because he felt such a keen responsibility for those workers who had served his family faithfully for years, as can be seen in his will:

> "[B]ut it is my desire that none of them should be sold without his or her consent, or in case of their misbehavior; except that infant children may be sold with their parent who consents for them to be sold with him or her, and who consents to be sold."

Sadly, Dolley would soon find herself solely responsible for Payne and his antics. Madison's health began to decline in the mid-1830s and she who had for so long been his hostess quietly slipped into the role of his nurse. When he died on June 28, 1836, she lost her best friend, confidant and protector. She would live the rest of her life in the shadow of the life they had enjoyed together, and it would now fall on her to maintain her husband's legacy for posterity while staving off financial disaster in the present.

Chapter 7: Dolley's Final Years

With her husband gone, Dolley threw herself into finishing his greatest work, the papers in which Madison gave his firsthand account of the Revolutionary period and the creation of the Constitution. With the help of her niece, Anna Payne, and the hindrance of her son, she managed to have the papers ready to sell to Congress by the end of 1837. The $30,000 she received for them had been intended by her husband to support her for the rest of her life. However, in no time at all Payne was again asking for money and Dolley was, as always, saying yes.

Blind to all his faults, she left Payne in charge of Montpelier that year and returned to Washington. Living in a house owned by her sister Anna (now Mrs. Richard Cutts), Dolley picked up where she'd left off in the Washington social scene. Her role as the only surviving widow of the Founding Fathers gave her a unique status, and she frequently entertained the Washington elite. No visit to the White House was complete without another to Dolley's little home across the square.

Again, Dolley's life would have been idyllic had it not been for her son. By this time Payne's body was showing the wear and tear of his profligate lifestyle, and without a firm, knowledgeable hand at the tiller, Montpelier declined steadily and ceased providing the income its 5,000 acres should have. In order to survive, Dolley next turned her eye toward selling her husband's papers. However, the entire Congress knew that any money they paid her would land in her son's pockets, so they refused.

Next, with a broken heart, she broke up the plantation in 1843 and sold part of it. With that infusion of cash, along with the rent she made from the mansion itself, she hoped to stay afloat. However, when she received a letter from one of her slaves warning that the sheriff was threatening to separate family members by selling them to a "negro buyer," she knew she had to act. She sold off the rest of the plantation in total, with the understanding that none of the slaves on the property would be sold without their own expressed permission.

In spite of personal tragedy, Dolley continued to enjoy entertaining others, and others began to draw upon her wealth of knowledge, especially incoming First Ladies. Dolley was sought out for advice by First Ladies Julia Tyler and Sarah Polk, as well as Priscilla Cooper Tyler, who served as the hostess for the invalid first Mrs. Tyler. Fittingly, Dolley's last public appearance was on the arm of President James Polk at his last White House reception.

In recognition of her personal character and her contribution to the nation, in 1848 Congress agreed to buy the rest of her husband's papers, with the stipulation that the $25,000 they paid her would be placed in trust and administered for her own care, not that of her son.

A daguerreotype of Dolley in 1848, by Mathew B. Brady

Dolley's special status among her contemporaries was evident in her final years. Dolley was given an honorary seat in Congress from which she could watch congressional debates from the floor, a nod to the fact that she was politically savvy and knowledgeable. Furthermore, when Samuel F.B. Morse invented the telegraph, he gave Dolley Madison the privilege of being the first private citizen to transmit a message via telegraph.

Unfortunately, Dolley had little time left to enjoy her new financial security. She fell very ill in July of 1849, and after less than a week confined to bed she passed away quietly on July 12. By order of the president, she was given a state funeral, with all of Washington in attendance, including President Zachary Taylor and most of his cabinet, as well as members of both houses of Congress, the Supreme Court and as many foreign diplomats as could make it to the service. She was initially buried in the Congressional Cemetery, but family members who knew her wished later had her reinterred by James at Montpelier.

Dolley's grave at Montpelier. Photo by Billy Hathorn

It is possible that during her 81 years of life, Dolley met more presidents than any other person in history. She personally knew every one of the first 12 presidents and had entertained or been entertained by most of them. She had also served as a trusted advisor to many of their wives, consulting with them on everything from diplomacy to recipes.

Of all the women who have every held the title of First Lady, none have done more to shape the very essence of the position more than Dolley Madison.

Bibliography

Allgor, Catherine. A Perfect Union: Dolley Madison and the Creation of the American Nation. New York: Holt Paperbacks (2007)

Cote, Richard N. Strength And Honor: The Life Of Dolley Madison. New York: Corinthian Books (2004)

Cutts, Lucia. Memoirs and Letters of Dolly Madison: Wife of James Madison, President of the United States New York: Nabu Press (2010)

Howard, Hugh. Mr. and Mrs. Madison's War: America's First Couple and the Second War of

Independence. New York: Bloomsbury Press (2012)

Lakkas, Chrisoula. Dolley Madison: More Than Just Ice Cream New York: Xlibris
Corporation (2010)

Mattern, David B. and Holly C. Shulman. The Selected Letters of Dolley Payne Madison.
Charlottesville: University of Virginia Press (2003)

Made in the USA
Lexington, KY
31 January 2016